What If My Kitty fasts in Ramadan

BY

RABIA GELGI

This book is dedicated to my children, and my amazing husband who's support made this happen.

Ramadan is a special and holy month that comes once in the Hijra calendar. It only lasts for a month. All Muslims fast during Ramadan. They neither eat nor drink from sunrise to sunset.

Everyone in the house prepares for Ramadan like there will be a party. Mom made to-do lists, prayer lists and gift lists. Then my brother and I decorated the house. Our Kitty was very happy to help us.

My dad told us that if anyone sees the crescent, also called the new moon, then Ramadan will begin.

"Can you see the new moon?" My brother said. "Yes!" We gladly replied. But kitty seemed very excited too.

Suhoor is an early breakfast before sunrise. I woke up at 3 o'clock Our Kitty seemed very sleepy. "My Kitty may not wake up for Suhoor. I whispered. "Wait, no!" she screamed, "how about my brother?"

After washing our hands and faces, we went to the to the breakfast table. Oh Allah! What a wonderful meal our mother had prepared for Suhoor.

We said 'Bismillah' and ate. "Eat as much as you can, Kitty!" I said. "It will be a long day tomorrow."

Finally Ramadan is here! We are very happy and curious about what our first fasting experience will be. I hope we make it till sunset.

My mom had prepared a jar for saving money for the whole month. At the end of the month, we will donate it to help the needy.

Time passed by very slow. We went to the kitchen and watched all the delicious foods. "Kitty, what do you think? Aren't these meals looking yummy?" I said. "We cannot eat them, we had promised." I added.

We are hungry, sleepy and tired. "Let's sleep and dream about the foods, Kitty!" I yelled.

Daddy had said Ramadan is the time to understand hungry people. I feel bad for them now.

Mom came into the room carrying soup bowls with great-smelling soup."You don't have to fast the whole day, little kids are allowed to eat." she said. "OK!" we giggled and smiled.

After eating, my brother said, "I swear that I have never eaten such a tasty soup." Mommy smiled and said, "The soup is the same as yesterday's"
But it seems our Kitty will not break it. "You are our super hero Kitty." I smiled.

"Oh Allah, please help hungry kids, they need some soup too. Our hearts are full of thanks that you have given us this delicious, tasty and yummy soup and we beg that you give the hungry kids some soup too." We prayed.

Ramadan is a month of Rahmah and Forgiveness; more generosity, more help, more kindness, more share and more thanks. So;

we planted trees

We prayed

We shared our belongings with friends

We donated foods

We shared our meals with our

neighbors.

Forgiveness

After all the activities, we had few minutes left to Iftar. Iftar is a meal that Muslims take when they want to break their fast. But even if we had broken our fasts, it was great to wait for Iftar. We watched the sunset from the window.

My parents prepared Iftar for our family and guests. "Our first guest of honor is Kitty." I said. "You deserve it." I added. We bought a gift for Kitty which had a big plate of fishes and four bottles of milk.

During Iftar, everybody says "Bismillah", and enjoy their meals. The food was simply delicious.

We went to the mosque together. Kitty did too. We met our friends there and we prayed to Allah for the blessings of the Holy Month.

Finally, the first day came to an end. We all went to bed tired but very happy to receive the month of Ramadan. We said "Alhamdulillah" for everything that we had today, and we said again to Kitty, "We are proud of you."

My Kitty was the hero of the first day of Ramadan. She got plenty of gifts and she shared her gifts with all of her friends. She is so kind.

CPSIA information can be obtained at www.ICGtesting.com
Printed in the USA
LVIW01n1304160518
577395LV00005B/23